As you begin to pay attention to your own

stories and what they say about you, you

will enter into the exciting process of becoming,

as you should be, the author of your own

life, the creator of your own possibilities.

MANDY AFTEL

ACKNOWLEDGEMENTS

WITH SPECIAL THANKS TO:

Jason Aldrich, Gerry Baird, Jay Baird, Neil Beaton, Josie Bissett, Jan Catey, Doug Cruickshank, Jim Darragh, Jennifer & Matt Ellison, Rob Estes, Michael Flynn & Family, Shannan Frisbie, Jennifer Hurwitz, Heidi Jones, Cristal & Brad Olberg, Janet Potter & Family, Diane Roger, Jenica Wilkie, Clarie Yam & Erik Lee, Kobi, Heidi & Shale Yamada, Justi, Tote & Caden Yamada, Robert & Val Yamada, Kaz, Kristin, Kyle & Kendyl Yamada, Tai & Joy Yamada, Anne Zadra, August & Arline Zadra.

CREDITS

Compiled by Kobi Yamada

Designed by Steve Potter

COURAGE every day.

COMPENDIUM™
PUBLISHING

live inspired.

Only those who
dare, truly live.

RUTH P. FREEDMAN

Finances

150.

Words.

Courage — As IF.

Laugh.

Rel.

Friends

Org.

reading
interests
stop — voice
record the good
meditate
cooking

Accept no one's
definition of your
life, define yourself.

HARVEY FIERSTEIN

COURAGE every day.

Courage is a
quality which
grows with use.

J.C. PENNEY

COURAGE every day.

Trust in your own
untried capacity.

ELLA WHEELER WILCOX

COURAGE every day.

What will you do
today that will
matter tomorrow?

RALPH MARSTON

COURAGE every day.

Anything's possible
if you've got
enough nerve.

J.K. ROWLING

COURAGE every day.

To have courage
for whatever comes
in life—everything
lies in that.

ST. TERESA OF AVILA

COURAGE every day.

There is a giant
asleep within every
person. When the
giant awakes,
miracles happen.

FREDERICK FAUST

COURAGE every day.

What a new face
courage puts on
everything.

RALPH WALDO EMERSON

COURAGE every day.

Boundaries
were meant
to be crossed.

KARI CASSIDY

COURAGE every day.

Our deeds
determine us,
as much as
we determine
our deeds.

GEORGE ELIOT

COURAGE every day.

Welcome problems
and eat them
for breakfast.

ALFRED A. MONTAPERT

COURAGE every day.

Life is about
becoming more
than we are.

OPRAH WINFREY

COURAGE every day.

The turning point
in the process of
growing up is when
you discover the
core of strength
within you that
survives all hurt.

MAX LERNER

COURAGE every day.

Each time you act
in spite of your
fear, you discover
even greater,
deeper courage.

ART BERG

COURAGE every day.

We cannot wait for
the storm to blow
over; we must learn
to work in the rain.

JENNIFER GRANHOLM

COURAGE every day.

When I let go
of what I am,
I become what
I might be.

LAO TZU

COURAGE every day.

Pessimists calculate
the odds. Optimists
believe they can
overcome them.

TED KOPPEL

COURAGE every day.

Behind the cloud
the sun is still
shining.

ABRAHAM LINCOLN

COURAGE every day.

What we have
before us are
some breathtaking
opportunities
disguised as
insoluble problems.

JOHN W. GARDNER

COURAGE every day.

Confront the
difficult while
it is still easy.

TAO TE CHING

COURAGE every day.

Understand there
are no guarantees,
make a bet on your
future, and then
throw everything
you got into it.

CATHY LARSON

COURAGE every day.

Some have thousands
of reasons why they
cannot do what they
want to, when all
they need is one
reason why they can.

WILLIS R. WHITNEY

COURAGE every day.

In our hands
is the power
to choose.

STEPHEN COVEY

COURAGE every day.

I think we should
follow a simple
rule: if we can
take the worst,
take the risk.

DR. JOYCE BROTHERS

COURAGE every day.

Decide to make
a dramatic move
that will change
everything for
the better.

KOBI YAMADA

COURAGE every day.

The bravest sight
in all this world is
someone fighting
against the odds.

FRANKLIN LANE

COURAGE every day.

Nothing in life
is to be feared,
it is only to be
understood. Now
is the time to
understand more,
so that we can
fear less.

MARIE CURIE

COURAGE every day.

The pain passes, but
the beauty remains.

PIERRE-AUGUSTE RENOIR

COURAGE every day.

There never was
night that had
no morn.

DINAH MULOCK CRAIK

COURAGE every day.

Turn a setback
into a comeback.

BILLY BREWER

COURAGE every day.

Let's dare to be
ourselves, for
we do that better
than anyone else.

SHIRLEY BRIGGS

COURAGE every day.

A small body
of determined
spirits fired by an
unquenchable faith
in their mission
can alter the
course of history.

MAHATMA GANDHI

COURAGE every day.

Leave your comfort
zone. Go stretch
yourself for a
good cause.

KOBI YAMADA

COURAGE every day.

The greatest test
of courage is to
bear defeat without
losing heart.

ROBERT G. INGERSOLL

COURAGE every day.

Overcoming the
unexpected and
discovering the
unknown is what
ignites our spirit.
It is what life is
all about.

DANIEL S. GOLDIN

COURAGE every day.

We must use time
creatively, and
forever realize that
the time is always
ripe to do right.

NELSON MANDELA

COURAGE every day.

Orville Wright
didn't have a
pilot's license.

RICHARD TATE

COURAGE every day.

The important
thing is this:
to be willing at
any moment to
sacrifice what we
are for what we
could become.

CHARLES DUBOIS

COURAGE every day.

Great hopes
make great lives.

DAN ZADRA

COURAGE every day.

We are the hurdles
we leap to be
ourselves.

MICHAEL McCLURE

COURAGE every day.

Every winner
has scars.

HERBERT N. CASSON

COURAGE every day.

Have the courage to
act instead of react.

DARLENE LARSON JENKS

COURAGE every day.

We define ourselves
by the best that
is in us, not the
worst that has
been done to us.

EDWARD LEWIS

COURAGE every day.

Life is the sum
of your choices.

ALBERT CAMUS

COURAGE every day.

Whatever my
individual desires
were to be free,
I was not alone.
There were many
others who felt
the same way.

ROSA PARKS

COURAGE every day.

What is at the
summit of courage,
I think, is freedom.

PAULA GIDDINGS

COURAGE every day.

Who dares wins.

If you haven't had
your life what
have you had?

HENRY JAMES

COURAGE every day.

We choose only
once. We choose
either to be
warriors or
to be ordinary.
A second choice
does not exist.
Not on this earth.

CARLOS CASTANEDA

COURAGE every day.

We are very near
to greatness: one
step and we are
safe; can we not
take the leap?

RALPH WALDO EMERSON

Let that which
stood in front go
behind! And let
that which was
behind advance to
the front and speak.

WALT WHITMAN

COURAGE every day.

Life is between
the trapeze bars.

HELEN KELLER

COURAGE every day.

I want to stay as
close to the edge
as I can without
going over. Out on
the edge you see
all kinds of things
you can't see from
the center.

KURT VONNEGUT

COURAGE every day.

We couldn't
possibly know
where it would
lead, but we knew
it had to be done.

BETTY FRIEDAN

COURAGE every day.

The human spirit
is stronger than
anything that can
happen to it.

GEORGE C. SCOTT

COURAGE every day.

It's hard to beat
a person who
never gives up.

BABE RUTH

COURAGE every day.

Suffering ceases
to be suffering in
some way at the
moment it finds
meaning.

VIKTOR FRANKL

COURAGE every day.

There will be only
one of you for all
time; fearlessly
be yourself.

UNKNOWN

COURAGE every day.

Do a little more
than you think
you possibly can.

LOWELL THOMAS

COURAGE every day.

In each of us are
places where we
have never gone.
Only by pressing
the limits do you
ever find them.

DR. JOYCE BROTHERS

COURAGE every day.

Heroes are the
people who do
what has to be
done when it
needs to be done,
regardless of the
consequences.

UNKNOWN

COURAGE every day.

You have to
expect things
of yourself before
you can do them.

MICHAEL JORDAN

COURAGE every day.

Where is the
university for
courage? The
university for
courage is to
do what you
believe in!

EL CORDOBÉS

COURAGE every day.

It takes an
uncommon amount
of guts to put your
dreams on the line,
to hold them up
and say, "How
good or how bad
am I?" That's where
courage comes in.

ERMA BOMBECK

COURAGE every day.

We acquire the
strength of that
which we have
overcome.

RALPH WALDO EMERSON

COURAGE every day.

If our civilization
has any hope of
survival, that hope
lies chiefly in what
we understand as
the human spirit.

VACLAV HAVEL

COURAGE every day.

No matter how
big and tough a
problem may be,
get rid of confusion
by taking one little
step toward solution.
Do something.

GEORGE NORDENHOLT

COURAGE every day.

Inside us there is
everything. We just
have to look for it.

JEFFERY RESSNER

COURAGE every day.

Things are only
impossible until
they're not.

JEAN-LUC PICARD

COURAGE every day.

Once you over-
come seemingly
insurmountable
obstacles, other
hurdles become
less daunting.

HOWARD SCHULTZ

COURAGE every day.

The most common
way people give
up their power is
by thinking they
don't have any.

ALICE WALKER

COURAGE every day.

Challenges make
you discover things
about yourself
that you never
really knew.

CICELY TYSON

COURAGE every day.

Our lives begin to
end the day we
become silent about
things that matter.

MARTIN LUTHER KING, JR.

COURAGE every day.

It only takes one
person to change
your life. You.

RUTH CASEY

COURAGE every day.

Dreams don't die
until we let them.

JAMES OJALA

COURAGE every day.

It seems to me
that people have
vast potential.
Most people can
do extraordinary
things if they have
the courage or
take the risks.

PHILIP ADAMS

COURAGE every day.

Hope unbelieved is
always considered
nonsense. But hope
believed is history
in the making.

JIM WALLIS

COURAGE every day.

Out of difficulties
we grow miracles.

JEAN DE LA BRUYERE

COURAGE every day.

You can't test
courage cautiously.

ANNIE DILLARD

COURAGE every day.

Show me a day
when the world
wasn't new.

SISTER BARBARA HANCE

COURAGE every day.

Difficulties exist to
be surmounted.

RALPH WALDO EMERSON

COURAGE every day.

A misty morning
does not signify
a cloudy day.

PROVERB

COURAGE every day.

We do not walk
on our legs, but
on our will.

SUFI PROVERB

COURAGE every day.

What would life
be like if we had
no courage to
attempt anything?

VINCENT VAN GOGH

COURAGE every day.

What you are
afraid to do is
a clear indicator
of the next thing
you need to do.

UNKNOWN

COURAGE every day.

Leap, and the net
will appear.

JULIA CAMERON

COURAGE every day.

When a great
adventure is offered,
you don't refuse it.

AMELIA EARHART

COURAGE every day.

You cannot discover
new oceans unless
you have the
courage to lose
sight of the shore.

DANIEL ABRAHAM

COURAGE every day.

We need heroes
because they draw
us on to become
better versions
of ourselves.

WALLY BOCK

COURAGE every day.

Action springs forth
not from thought,
but from a readiness
for responsibility.

DIETRICH BONHOEFFER

COURAGE every day.

Don't let your fear
grow bigger than
your faith.

JOSIE BISSETT

COURAGE every day.

Temporary setbacks
are simply part of
the equation.

BOB MOAWAD

COURAGE every day.

The world is divided
into two classes,
those who believe
the incredible, and
those who do the
improbable.

OSCAR WILDE

COURAGE every day.

Success can only
be measured in
terms of distance
traveled.

MAVIS GALLANT

COURAGE every day.

I have simply tried
to do what seemed
best each day, as
each day came.

ABRAHAM LINCOLN

COURAGE every day.

As you battle for
strength and courage
and healing, remember:
there are people all
around you cheering
you on and waiting
to lend a hand.

KATHRYN T. SHAW

COURAGE every day.

Depend upon it,
the lovers of
freedom will
be free.

EDMUND BURKE

COURAGE every day.

If you hear a
voice within you
say, "you cannot
paint," then by
all means paint,
and that voice
will be silenced.

VINCENT VAN GOGH

COURAGE every day.

The very least
you can do in your
life is to figure
out what you hope
for. And the most
you can do is live
inside that hope.

BARBARA KINGSOLVER

COURAGE every day.

There is a power
now slumbering
within us, which if
awakened would do
to evil what light
does to darkness.

MAHATMA GANDHI

COURAGE every day.

Here's to the pilot
that weathered
the storm.

GEORGE CANNING

COURAGE every day.

Freedom is not
worth having if it
does not include
the freedom to
make mistakes.

MAHATMA GANDHI

COURAGE every day.

Any life, no matter
how long and
complex it may be,
is made up of a single
moment—the moment
in which a man finds
out, once and for all,
who he is.

JORGE LUIS BORGES

COURAGE every day.

Behind all this,
some great
happiness is
hiding.

YEHUDA AMICHAI

COURAGE every day.

Never deny a
diagnosis, but do
deny the negative
verdict that may
go with it.

NORMAN COUSINS

COURAGE every day.

Little minds are
tamed and subdued
by misfortune;
but great minds
rise above them.

WASHINGTON IRVING

COURAGE every day.

Life has no
romance
without risk.

SARAH DOHERTY

COURAGE every day.

To fear is to
expect punishment.
To love is to know
we are immersed
not in darkness,
but in light.

MOTHER TERESA

COURAGE every day.

Come, my friends.
'Tis not too late to
make a newer world.

ALFRED, LORD TENNYSON